Crocodiles and Noodles

A Collection of Themed Poems

Heinemann
LIBRARY

H www.heinemann.co.uk

Visit our website to find out more information about **Heinemann Library** books.

To order:

☎ Phone 44 (0) 1865 888066

▤ Send a fax to 44 (0) 1865 314091

▢ Visit the Heinemann Bookshop at www.heinemann.co.uk to browse our catalogue and order online.

First published in Great Britain by Heinemann Library, Halley Court, Jordan Hill, Oxford OX2 8EJ, a division of Reed Educational and Professional Publishing Ltd. Heinemann is a registered trademark of Reed Educational & Professional Publishing Limited.

OXFORD MELBOURNE AUCKLAND JOHANNESBURG BLANTYRE
GABORONE IBADAN PORTSMOUTH NH (USA) CHICAGO

Originated by Dot Gradations Ltd, Wickford
Printed in Hong Kong

04 03 02 01 00
10 9 8 7 6 5 4 3 2 1

ISBN 0 431 07509 3
This title is also available in a big book edition 0 431 07410 0

British Library Cataloguing in Publication Data
Crocodiles & Noodles: a collection of themed poems. – (Poetry Hour)
1. Children's poetry, English
I. Martin, Peggy-Lou
821'.008

Acknowledgements
Ian Beck, pp4, 12; Rebecca Wildsmith, pp5, 7; Cathy Baxter, p6; Nicki Palin, pp8-9, 30; Allan Curless, pp10-11; John Taylor, p.13; Satoshi Kitamura, pp16-17, 29; Jan Lewis, p18; Pat Ludlow, p.20-21; Alan Marks, p22; Alex de Wolf, p23, 26-27, 31; Jane Bottomley, pp24-25.

The Duck by Ogden Nash, from 'Verses from 1929 On' by Ogden Nash. Copyright © 1936 by Ogden Nash, first appeared in The Saturday Evening Post. By permission of Little, Brown and Company (Inc). USA, Philippines and Canada. 'The Duck' by Ogden Nash, from 'Candy is Dandy: The Best of Ogden Nash', published by Andre Deutsch Ltd. Reprinted by permission of Andre Deutsch Ltd - UK & Comm excl Canada; **On The Ning Nang Nong** by Spike Milligan. Reprinted by permission of Spike Milligan Productions Limited; **The Flattered Flying Fish** by E. V. Rieu. Reprinted by permission of the Estate of E. V. Rieu; Extract from **The Bed Book** by Sylvia Plath, published by Faber and Faber Limited. Reprinted by permission of the publisher; **Countdown** by Jack Prelutsky, from 'It's

Halloween, © Jack Prelutsky 1977. Published by Mammoth, an imprint of Egmont Children's Books Limited, London, and used with permission. Also reprinted by permission of HarperCollins Publishers Inc, for USA; **Bedtime** by Allan Ahlberg, from 'Please Mrs Butler' by Allan Ahlberg (Kestrel 1983) (pg 93, 12 lines), Copyright © Allan Ahlberg, 1983. Reprinted by permission of Penguin Books Limited; **The Horseman** by Walter de la Mare, from 'The Complete Poems of Walter de la Mare'. Reprinted by permission of The Literary Trustees of Walter de la Mare, and the Society of Authors as their representatives; **Tickling** by Theresa Heine. Reprinted by permission of the author; **This is the Hand** by Michael Rosen, published by Scholastic Children's Books Limited; **New Shoes** by John Agard, from 'I Din Do Nuttin', published by The Bodley Head. Reprinted by permission of The Random House Group Limited, on behalf of John Agard; **Spaghetti** by Shel Silverstein, from 'Where The Sidewalk Ends' by Shel Silverstein Copyright 1974 by Evil Eye Music Inc. By permission of Edite Kroll Literary Agency Inc, and also with permission of HarperCollins Publishers Inc, for USA; **If I Were King** by A. A. Milne, from 'When We Were Very Young' by A. A. Milne. Copyright under the Berne Convention. Published by Methuen, an imprint of Egmont Children's Books Limited, London, and used with permission. 'If I Were King' by A. A. Milne, from 'When We Were Very Young' by A. A. Milne copyright 1924 by E. P. Dutton, renewed 1952 by A. A. Milne. Used by permission of Dutton Children's Books, a division of Penguin Putnam Inc.

Poetry Hour is a version of selected poems from Heinemann Primary's Poetry Parade.

Contents

Pussy cat, Pussy cat

a traditional rhyme

Pussy cat, pussy cat,
Where have you been?
I've been to London
To look at the Queen.
Pussy cat, pussy cat,
What did you there?
I frightened a little mouse
Under her chair.

How Doth
The Little Crocodile
by Lewis Carroll

How doth the little crocodile
   Improve his shining tail,
And pour the waters of the Nile
   On every golden scale!

How cheerfully he seems to grin,
   How neatly spreads his claws,
And welcomes little fishes in,
   With gently smiling jaws!

Through the Jungle

a rhyme from India

Through the jungle the elephant goes,
Swaying his trunk to and fro,
Munching, crunching, tearing trees,
Stamping seeds, eating leaves.
His eyes are small, his feet are fat,
Hey, elephant, don't behave like that.

The Duck

by Ogden Nash

Behold the duck.
It does not cluck.
A cluck it lacks.
It quacks.
It is specially fond
Of a puddle or pond.
When it dines or sups,
It bottoms ups.

On the Ning Nang Nong
by Spike Milligan

On the Ning Nang Nong
Where the Cows go Bong!
And the Monkeys all say Boo!
There's a Nong Nang Ning
Where the trees go Ping!
And the tea pots Jibber Jabber Joo.
On the Nong Ning Nang
All the mice go Clang!
And you just can't catch 'em when they do!
So it's Ning Nang Nong!
Cows go Bong!
Nong Nang Ning!
Trees go Ping!
Nong Ning Nang!
The mice go Clang!
What a noisy place to belong,
Is the Ning Nang Ning Nang Nong!!

The Flattered Flying-Fish
by E. V. Rieu

Said the Shark to the Flying-Fish over the phone:
"Will you join me to-night? I am dining alone.
Let me order a nice little dinner for two!
And come as you are, in your shimmering blue."

Said the Flying-Fish: "Fancy remembering me,
And the dress that I wore at the Porpoises' tea!"
"How could I forget?" said the Shark in his guile:
"I expect you at eight!" and rang off with a smile.

She has powdered her nose; she has put on her things;
She is off with one flap of her luminous wings.
O little one, lovely, light-hearted and vain,
The Moon will not shine on your beauty again!

Little Boy Blue

a traditional rhyme

Little Boy Blue,
Come blow your horn,
The sheep's in the meadow,
The cow's in the corn.
Where is the boy
Who looks after the sheep?
He's under a haycock
Fast asleep.
Will you wake him?
No, not I,
For if I do,
He's sure to cry.

There Was An Old Man With A Beard

by Edward Lear

There was an Old Man with a beard,
Who said, "It is just as I feared! —
   Two Owls and a Hen,
   Four Larks and a Wren,
Have all built their nests in my beard!"

Solomon Grundy

a traditional rhyme

Solomon Grundy,

Born on a Monday,

Christened on Tuesday,

Married on Wednesday,

Took ill on Thursday,

Worse on Friday,

Died on Saturday,

Buried on Sunday.

This is the end
Of Solomon Grundy.

Extract from **The Bed Book**
by *Sylvia Plath*

Beds come in all sizes –
Single or double,
Cot-size or cradle,
King-size or trundle.

Most Beds are Beds
For sleeping or resting,
But the *best* Beds are much
More interesting!

Not just a white little
Tucked-in-tight little
Nighty-night little
Turn-out-the-light little
Bed –

Instead
A Bed for Fishing,
A Bed for Cats,
A Bed for a Troupe of
Acrobats.

The *right* sort of Bed
(If you see what I mean)
Is a Bed that might
Be a Submarine

Nosing through water
Clear and green,
Silver and glittery
As a sardine

Or a Jet-Propelled Bed
For visiting Mars
With mosquito nets
For the shooting stars . . .

Countdown
by Jack Prelutsky

There are ten ghosts in the pantry,
There are nine upon the stairs,
There are eight ghosts in the attic,
There are seven on the chairs,
There are six within the kitchen,
There are five along the hall,
There are four upon the ceiling,
There are three upon the wall,
There are two ghosts on the carpet,
Doing things that ghosts will do,
There is one ghost right behind me
Who is oh so quiet . . . BOO.

Bedtime

by Allan Ahlberg

When I go upstairs to bed,
I usually give a loud cough.
This is to scare The Monster off.

When I come to my room,
I usually slam the door right back.
This is to squash The Man in Black
Who sometimes hides there.

Nor do I walk to the bed,
But usually run and jump instead.
This is to stop The Hand –
Which is under there all right –
From grabbing my ankles.

Hush Little Baby

an Afro-American lullaby

Hush, little baby, don't say a word,
Papa's going to buy you a mocking bird.

If that mocking bird won't sing,
Papa's going to buy you a diamond ring.

If the diamond ring turns to brass,
Papa's going to buy you a looking-glass.

If the looking-glass gets broke,
Papa's going to buy you a billy-goat.

If that billy-goat runs away,
Papa's going to buy you another today.

The Horseman
by Walter de la Mare

I heard a horseman
　　Ride over the hill;
The moon shone clear,
The night was still;
His helm was silver,
　　And pale was he;
And the horse he rode
　　Was of ivory.

Tickling

by Theresa Heine

He giggles and squeaks,
And wriggles and cries,
And curls and rolls,
And screws up his eyes,
And squirms and squeals,
And shouts and yells,
And screeches and begs,
And bangs his legs,
Till mum puts her head
Round the door and says,
"Stop tickling your brother!"

This is the Hand
by Michael Rosen

This is the hand
that touched the frost
that froze my tongue
and made it numb

this is the hand
that cracked the nut
that went in my mouth
and never came out

this is the hand
that slid round the bath
to find the soap
that wouldn't float

this is the hand
on the hot water bottle
meant to warm my bed
that got lost instead

this is the hand
that held the bottle
that let go of the soap
that cracked the nut
that touched the frost
this is the hand
that never gets lost.

New Shoes

by John Agard

Buying new shoes
takes so long.
When the colour is right
the size is wrong.

The lady asks
How does it fit?
I say to Mum
Pinches a bit.

But that's not true
It's just because
I don't want the brown
I prefer the blue.

The lady goes inside
brings another size
this time the blue.
Not too big. Not too tight.

As you guessed
Just right, just right.
Mum says, "The blue will do."
And I agree. Don't you?

Spaghetti

by Shel Silverstein

Spaghetti, spaghetti, all over the place,
Up to my elbows – up to my face,
Over the carpet and under the chairs,
Into the hammock and wound round the stairs,
Filling the bathtub and covering the desk,
Making the sofa a mad mushy mess.

The party is ruined, I'm terribly worried,
The guests have all left (unless they're all buried).
I told them, "Bring presents." I said, "Throw confetti."
I guess they heard wrong
'Cause they all threw spaghetti!

Oodles of Noodles

by Lucia and James L. Hymes, Jr.

I love noodles. Give me oodles.
Make a mound up to the sun.
Noodles are my favourite foodles.
I eat noodles by the ton.

I Had A Little Nut Tree

a traditional rhyme

I had a little nut tree,
Nothing would it bear
But a silver nutmeg
And a golden pear;
The king of Spain's daughter
Came to visit me,
And all for the sake
Of my little nut tree.
I skipped over water,
I danced over sea,
And all the birds in the air
Couldn't catch me.

If I Were King

by A. A. Milne

I often wish I were a King,
And then I could do anything.

If only I were King of Spain,
I'd take my hat off in the rain.

If only I were King of France,
I wouldn't brush my hair for aunts.

I think, if I were King of Greece,
I'd push things off the mantelpiece.

If I were King of Norroway,
I'd ask an elephant to stay.

If I were King of Babylon,
I'd leave my button gloves undone.

If I were King of Timbuctoo,
I'd think of lovely things to do.

If I were King of anything,
I'd tell the soldiers, "I'm the King!"

Index of first lines